MW01116480

ONE LYFE MEDIA

COMMITMENT TO COMMUNITY

This chapter is the first of many chapters within this series.

We intend to share our unique experiences to help our community deepen its understanding of personal finance and encourage healthy financial habits through easy-to-digest content.

Each character featured in our comics is on a journey, and we hope that sharing that journey helps our community to dream big and achieve its financial goals.
What's your dream?

www.OneLyfeMedia.com
info@onelyfemedia.com

BASED ON A TRUE STORY

www.OneLyfeMedia.com
info@onelyfemedia.com

THE CAR CHAPTER

It's a nice summer day in Queens, NY. Lyfe is with his friend Promise and wants to buy a car so he can live off campus when he returns to college in the fall.

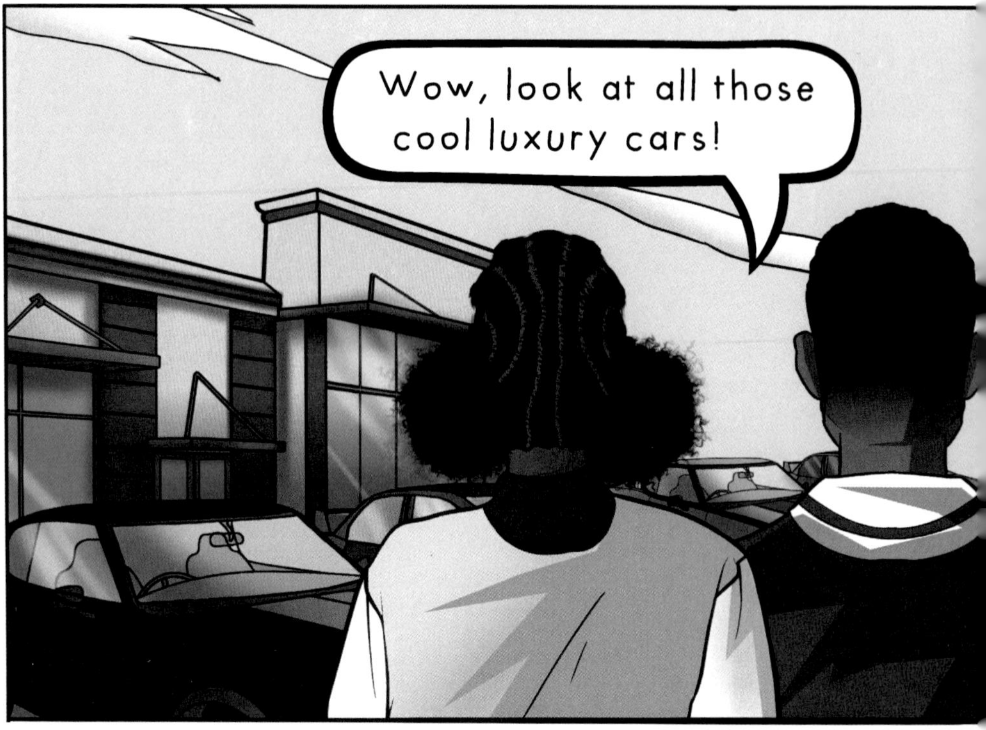
Wow, look at all those cool luxury cars!

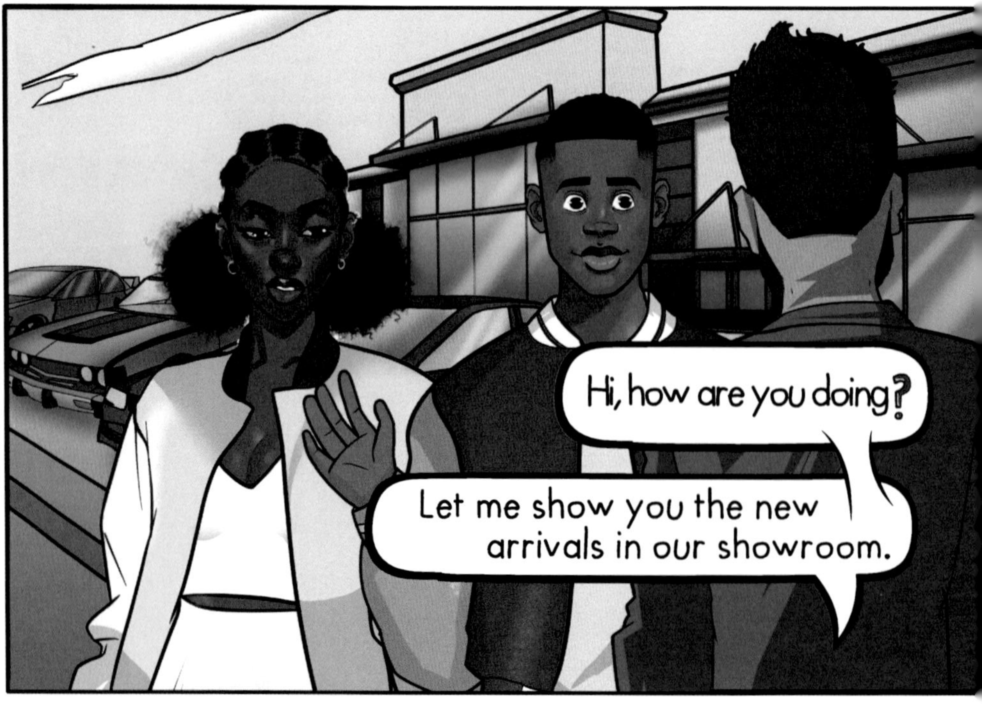
Hi, how are you doing?
Let me show you the new arrivals in our showroom.

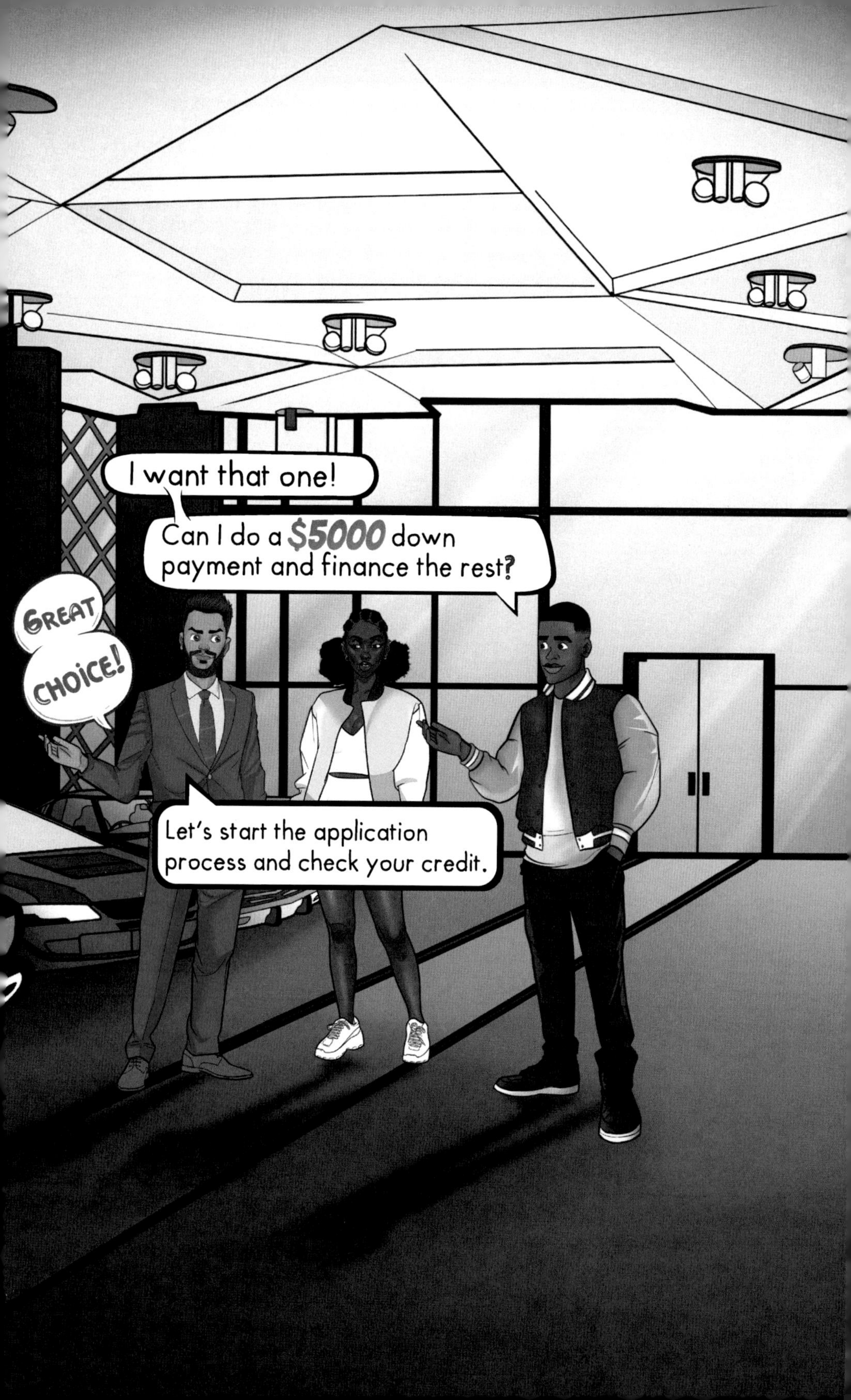
I want that one!
Can I do a $5000 down payment and finance the rest?
GREAT CHOICE!
Let's start the application process and check your credit.

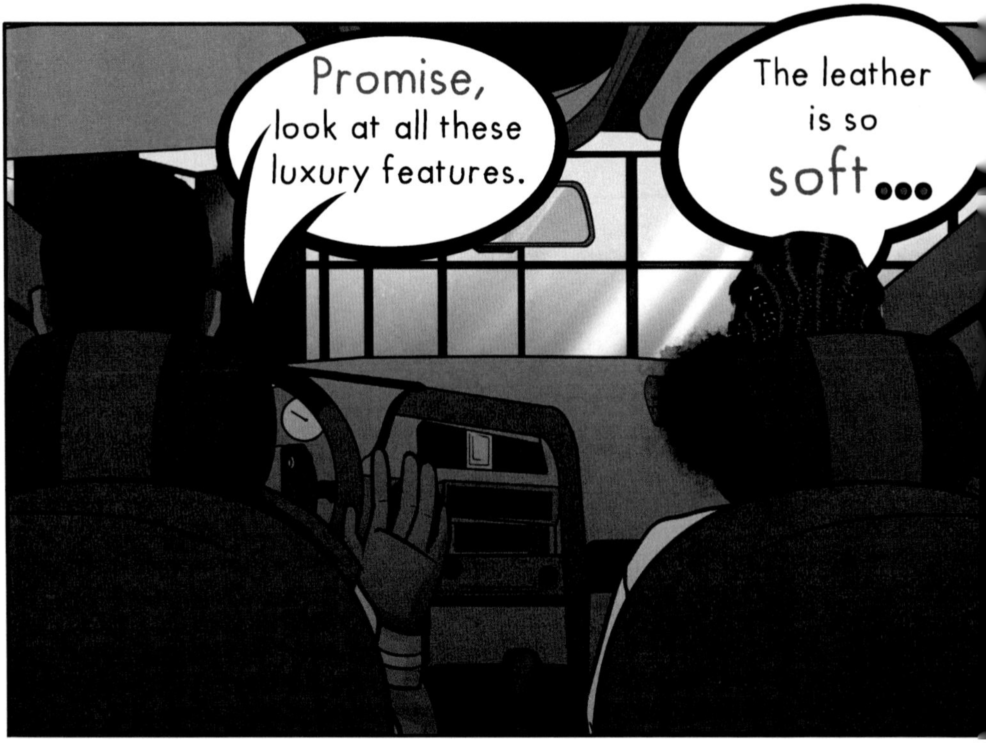
Promise, look at all these luxury features.
The leather is so soft...

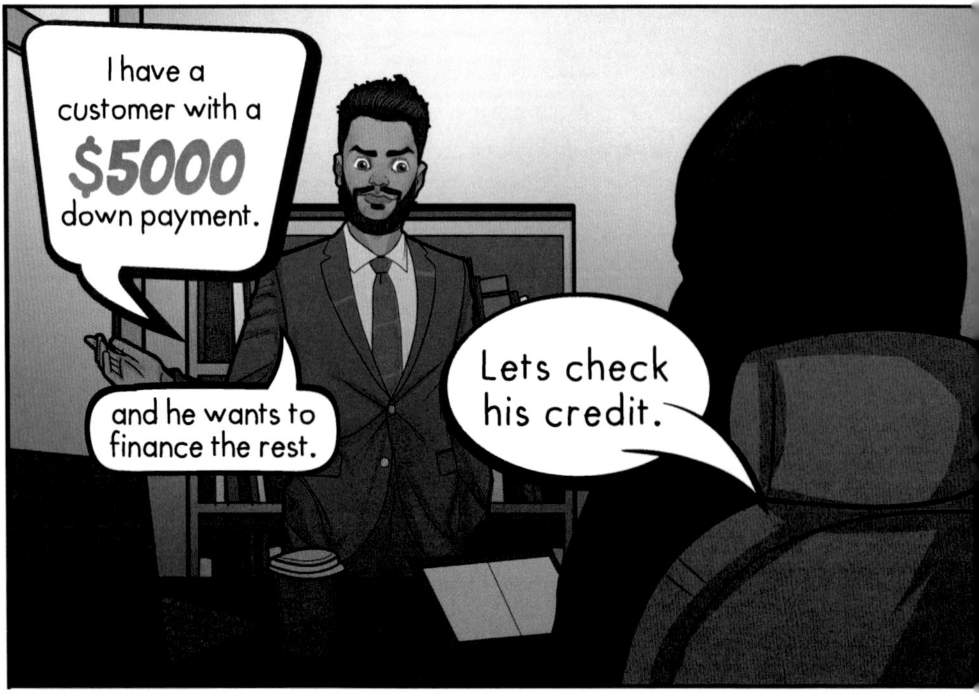
I have a customer with a $5000 down payment.
and he wants to finance the rest.
Lets check his credit.

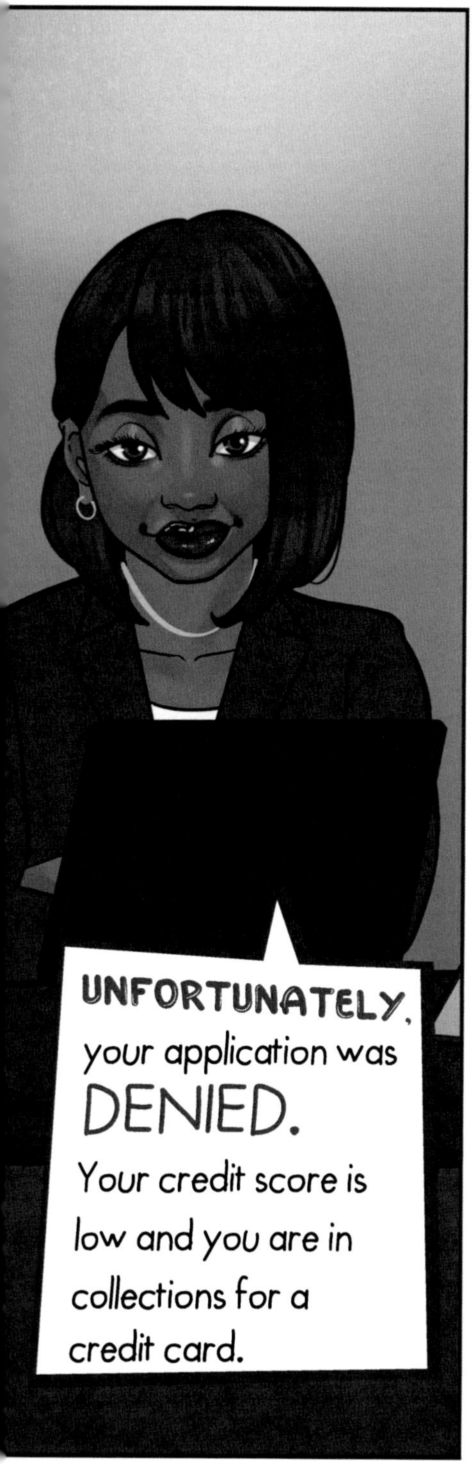
UNFORTUNATELY, your application was DENIED. Your credit score is low and you are in collections for a credit card.

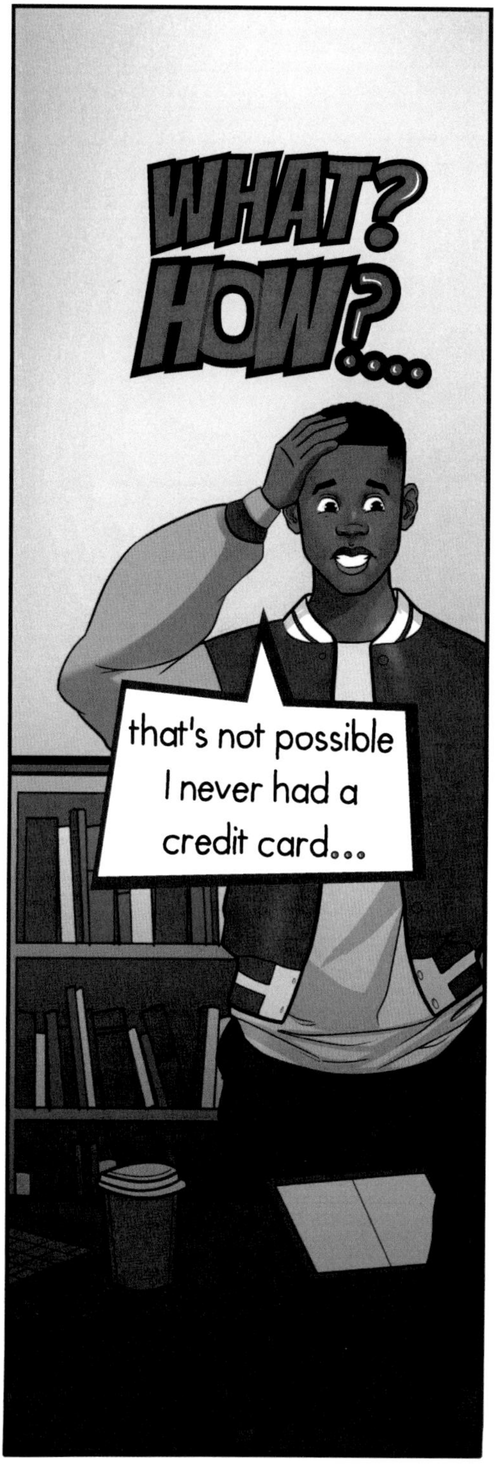
WHAT? HOW?....
that's not possible I never had a credit card...

Two years prior,
while Lyfe was in college,
a credit card representative
approached Lyfe. However, he
did not know how credit worked.
He had no idea he had to pay
his credit line off.

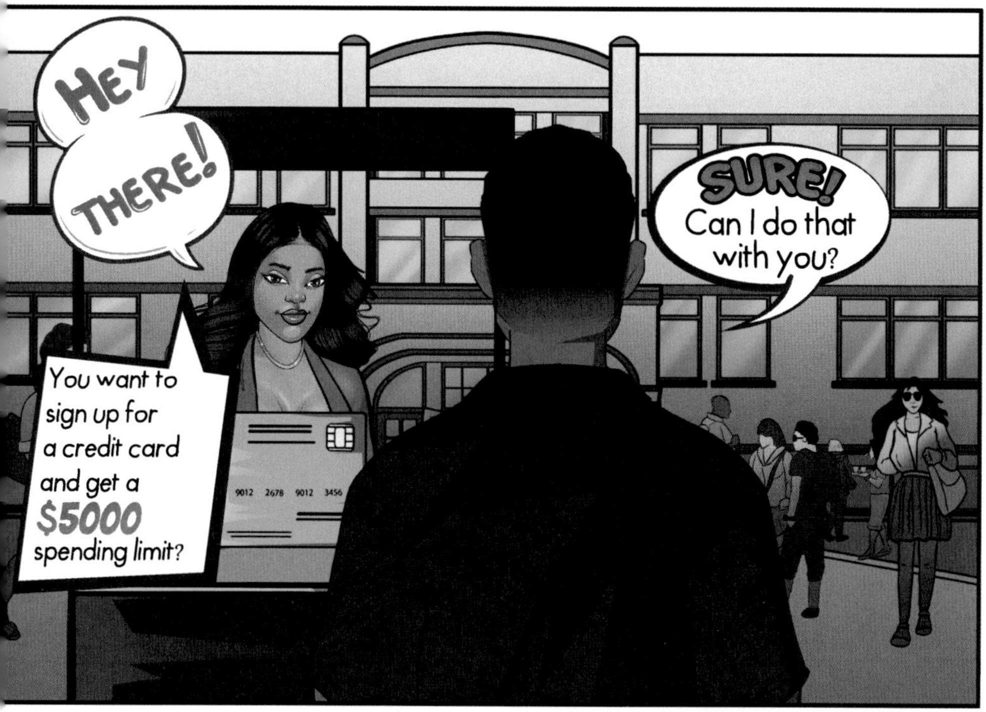
HEY THERE!
You want to sign up for a credit card and get a $5000 spending limit?
SURE! Can I do that with you?
9012 2678 9012 3456

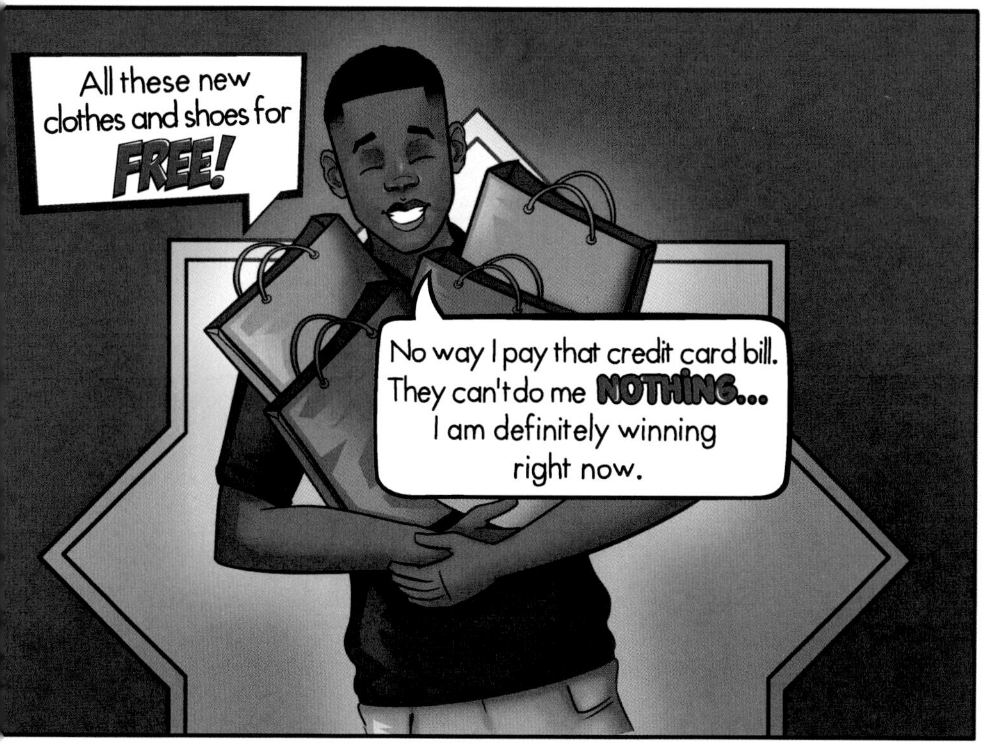
All these new clothes and shoes for FREE!
No way I pay that credit card bill. They can't do me NOTHING... I am definitely winning right now.

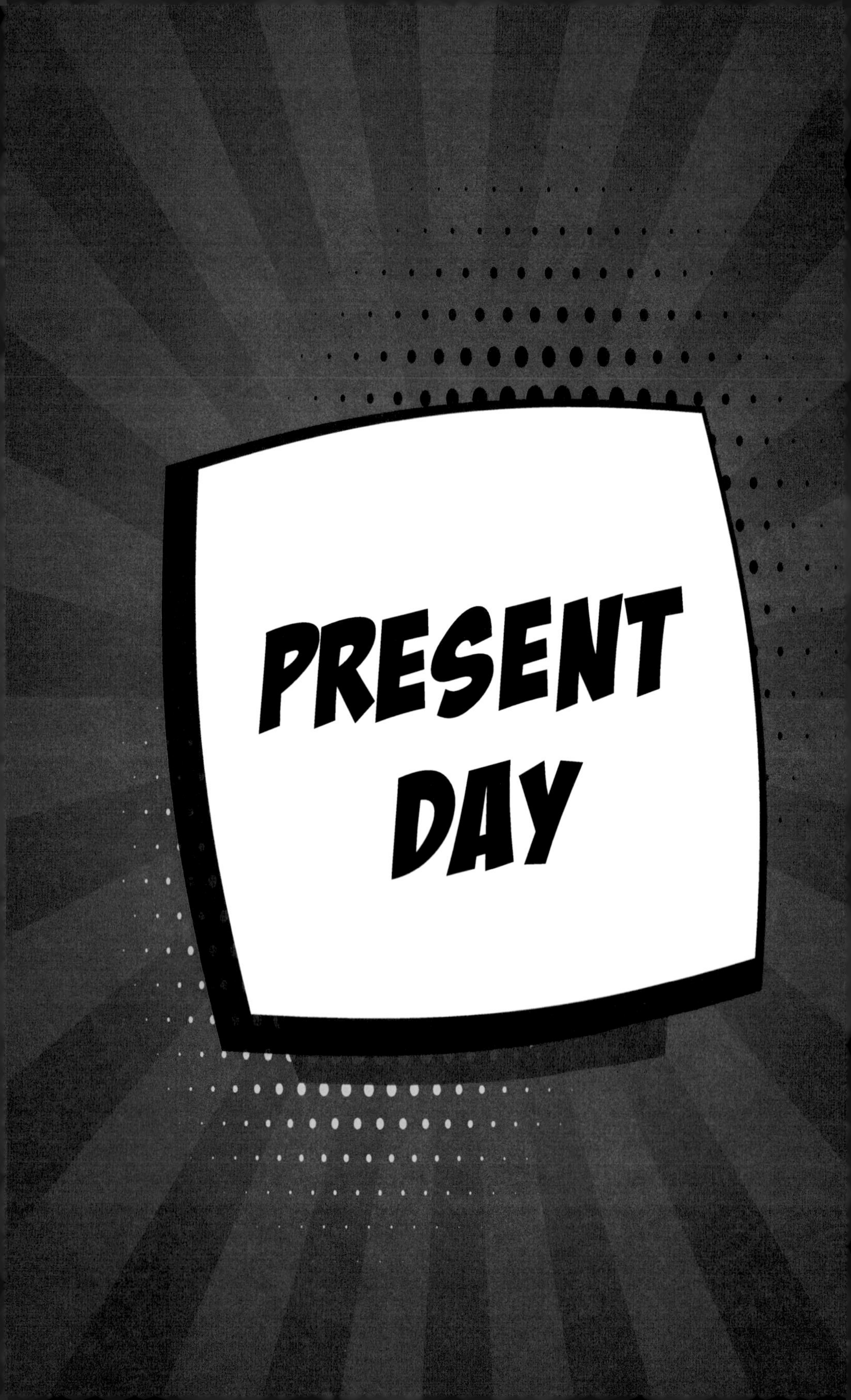
PRESENT DAY

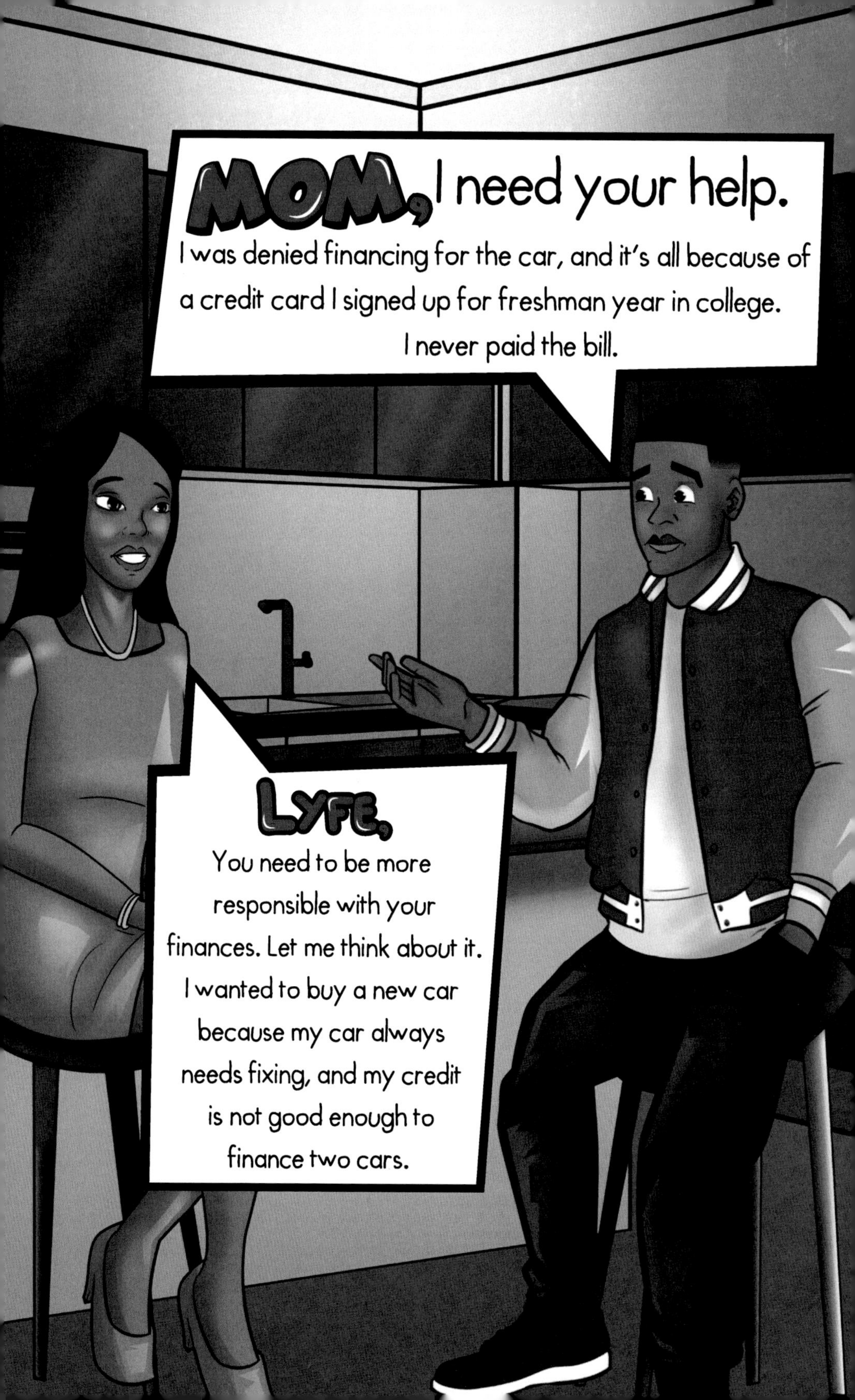
MOM, I need your help.
I was denied financing for the car, and it's all because of a credit card I signed up for freshman year in college. I never paid the bill.
LYFE,
You need to be more responsible with your finances. Let me think about it. I wanted to buy a new car because my car always needs fixing, and my credit is not good enough to finance two cars.

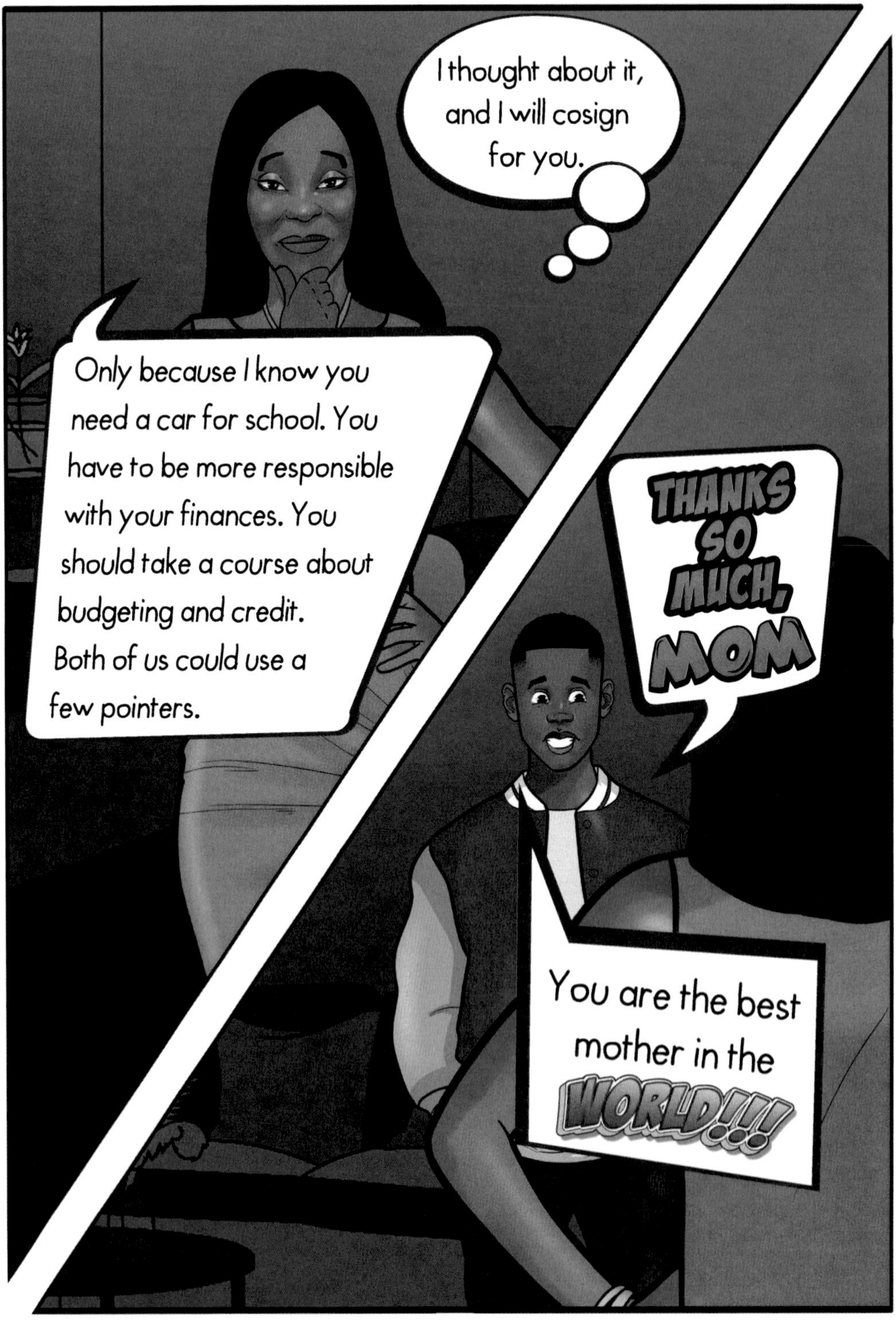
I thought about it, and I will cosign for you.
Only because I know you need a car for school. You have to be more responsible with your finances. You should take a course about budgeting and credit. Both of us could use a few pointers.
THANKS SO MUCH, MOM
You are the best mother in the WORLD!!!

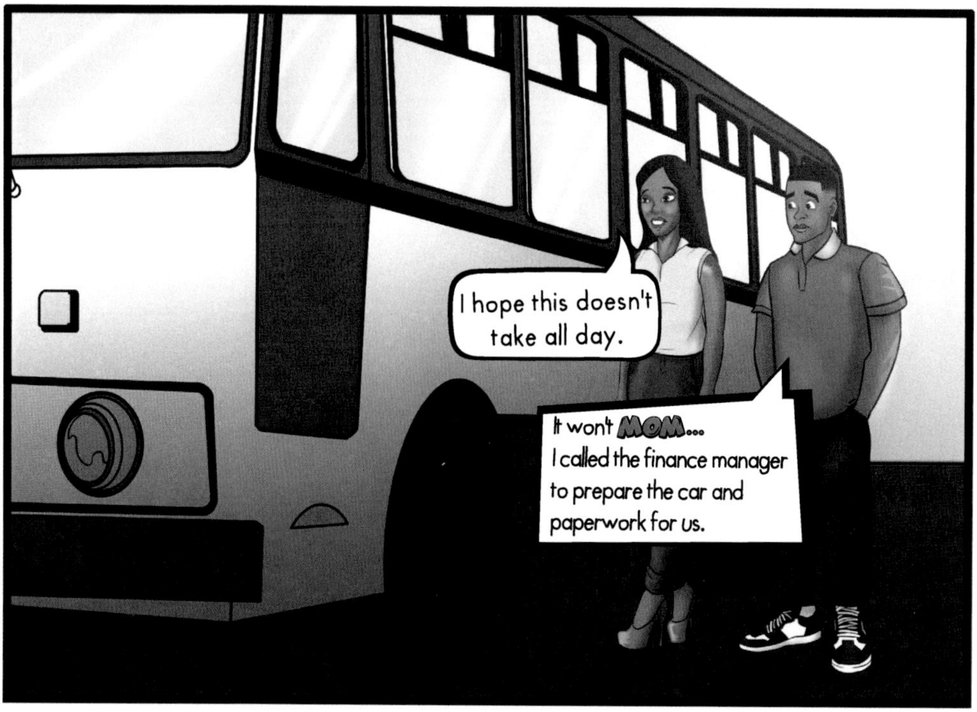
I hope this doesn't take all day.
It won't MOM...
I called the finance manager to prepare the car and paperwork for us.

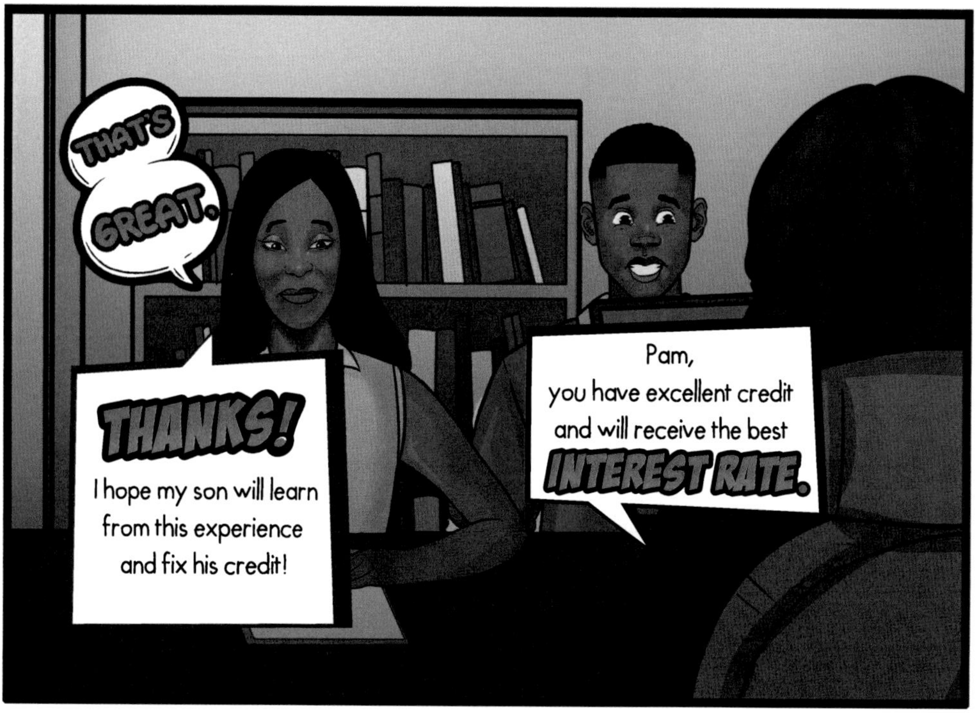
THAT'S GREAT.
Pam,
you have excellent credit and will receive the best INTEREST RATE.
THANKS!
I hope my son will learn from this experience and fix his credit!

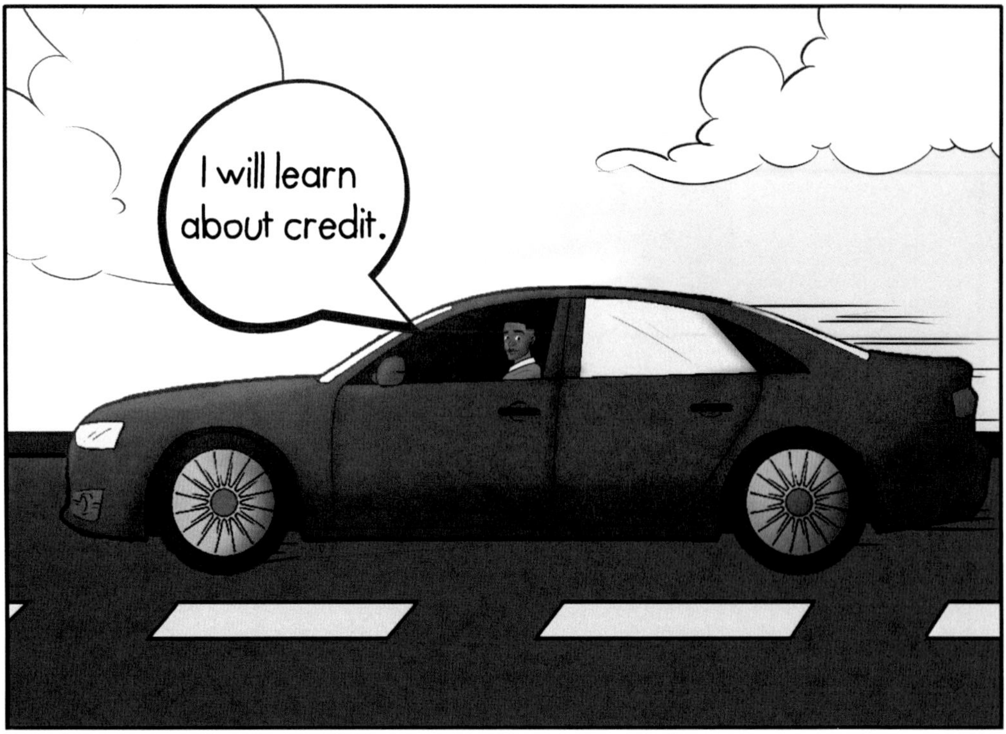
I will learn about credit.

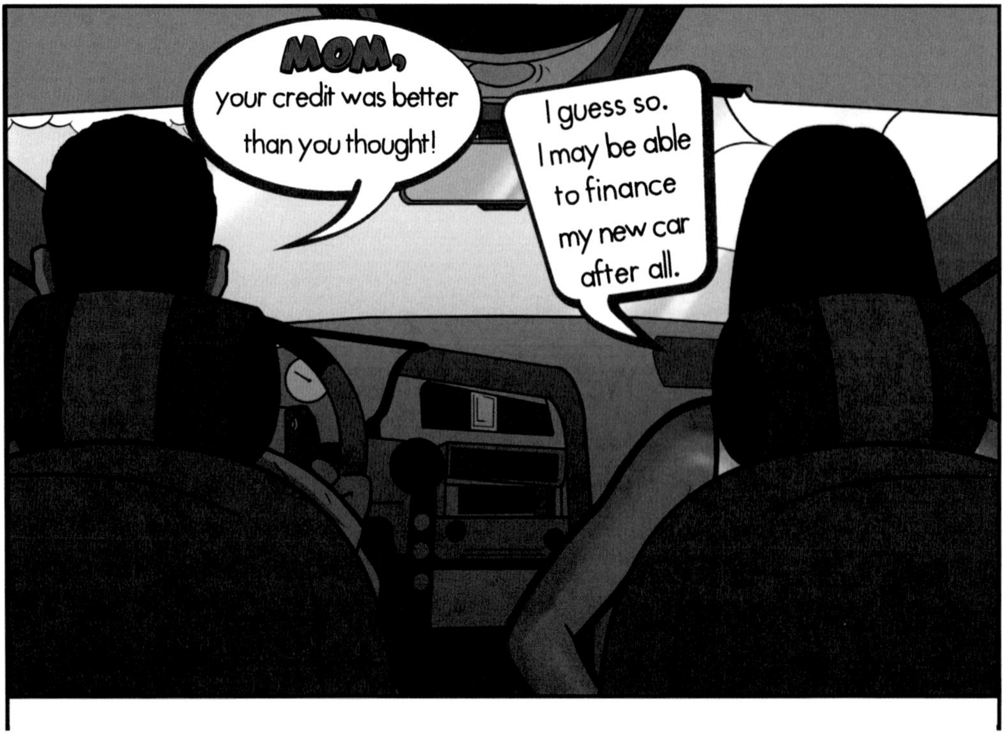
MOM, your credit was better than you thought!
I guess so. I may be able to finance my new car after all.

ALTERNATE ENDING

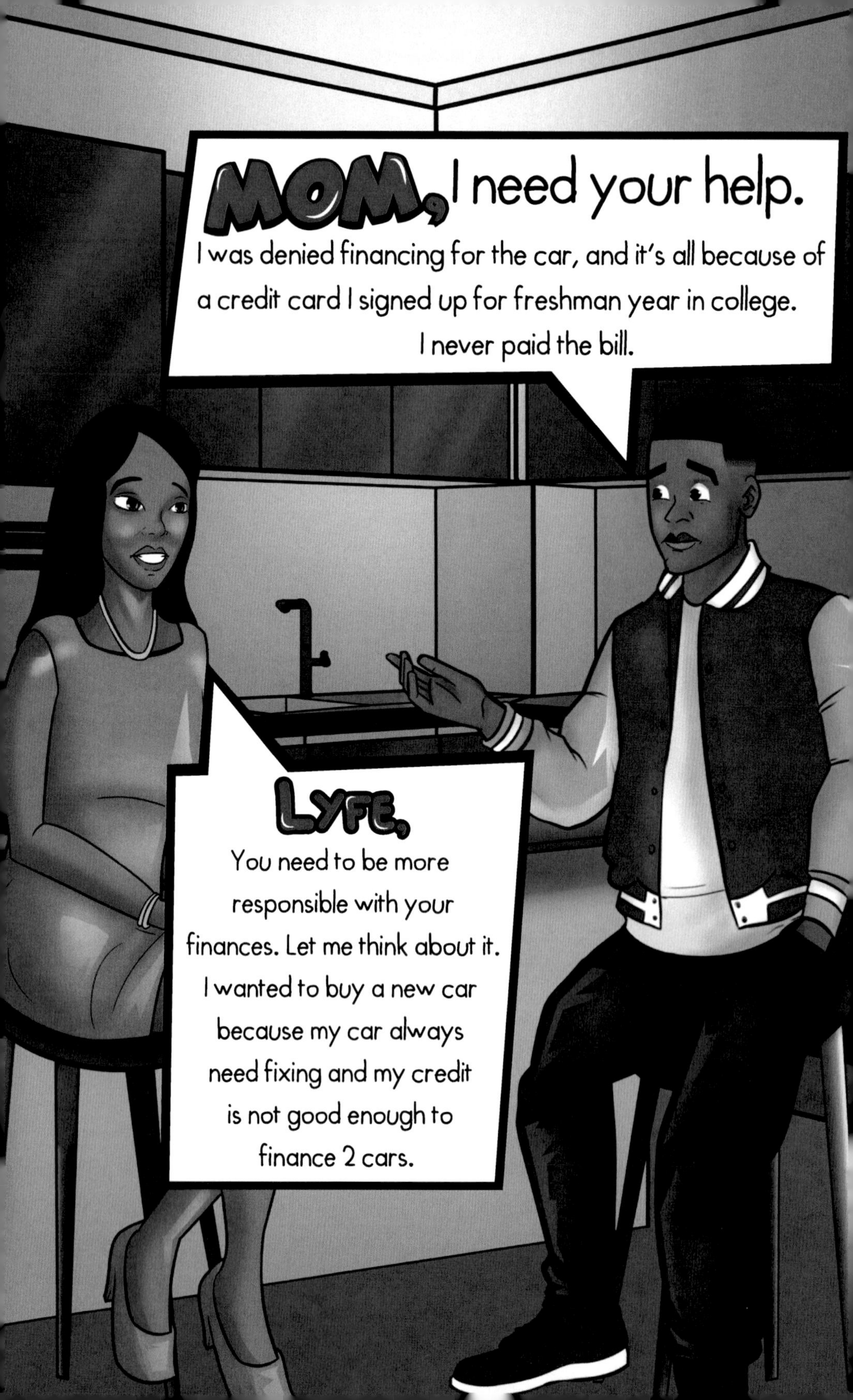
MOM, I need your help.
I was denied financing for the car, and it's all because of a credit card I signed up for freshman year in college. I never paid the bill.
LYFE,
You need to be more responsible with your finances. Let me think about it. I wanted to buy a new car because my car always need fixing and my credit is not good enough to finance 2 cars.

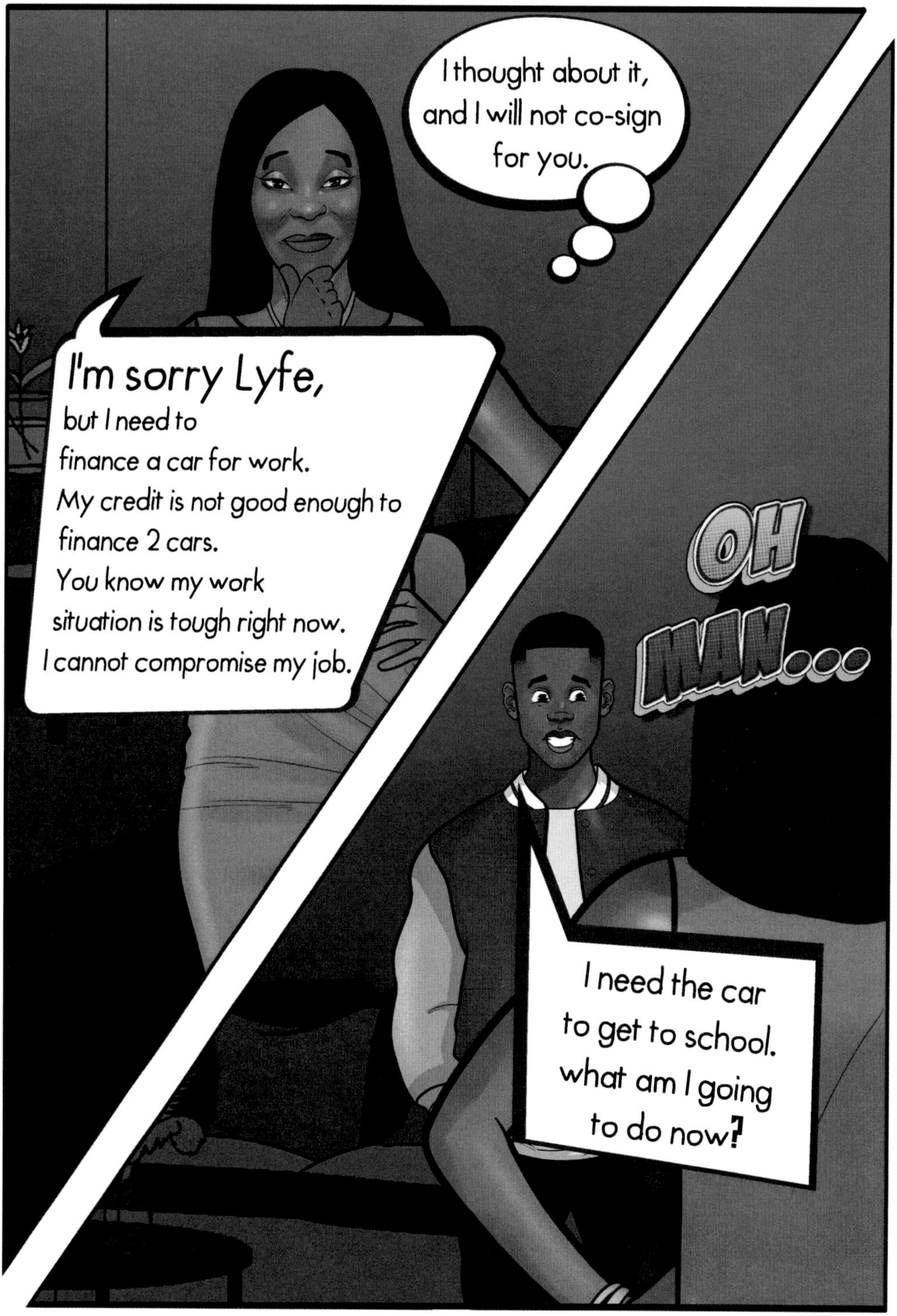
I thought about it, and I will not co-sign for you.
I'm sorry Lyfe, but I need to finance a car for work. My credit is not good enough to finance 2 cars. You know my work situation is tough right now. I cannot compromise my job.
OH MAN...
I need the car to get to school. what am I going to do now?

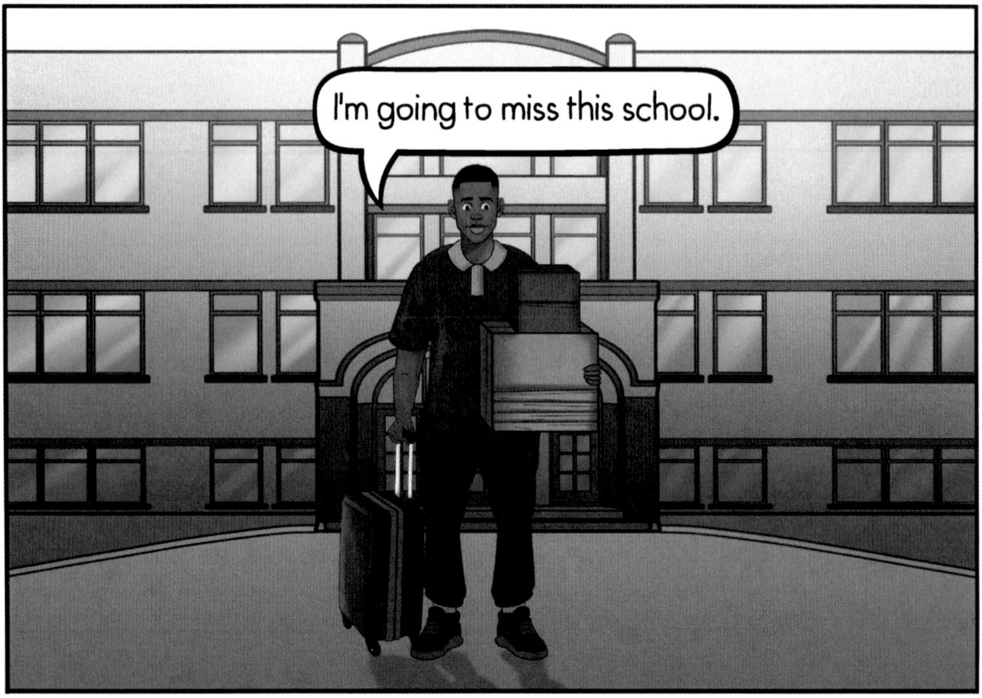
I'm going to miss this school.

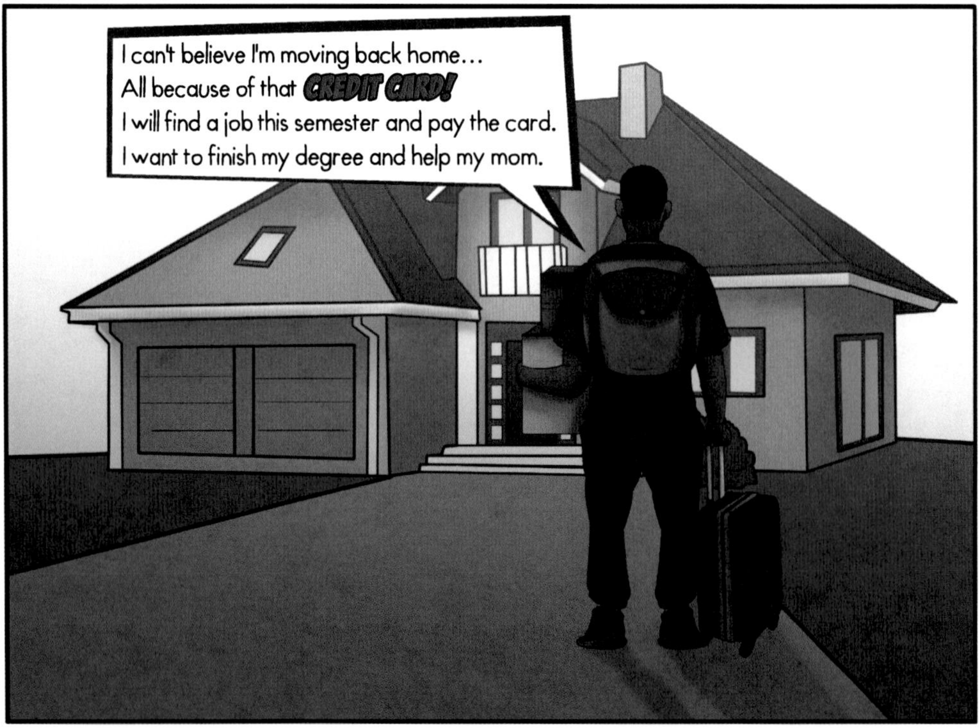
I can't believe I'm moving back home...
All because of that CREDIT CARD!
I will find a job this semester and pay the card.
I want to finish my degree and help my mom.

FOUR LESSONS

1. What is credit?

2. What is a credit score?

3. What is interest?

4. Why should I pay
my balance in full & on-time?

WHAT IS CREDIT?

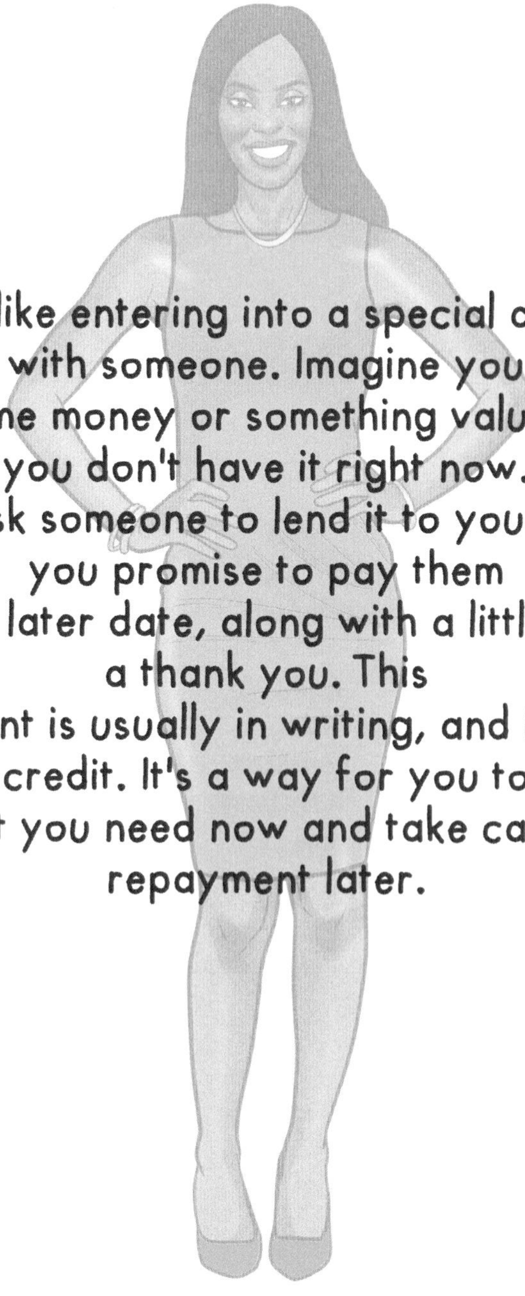

Credit is like entering into a special agreement with someone. Imagine you need some money or something valuable, but you don't have it right now. So, you ask someone to lend it to you. In return, you promise to pay them back at a later date, along with a little extra as a thank you. This agreement is usually in writing, and it's called credit. It's a way for you to get what you need now and take care of the repayment later.

WHAT IS A CREDIT SCORE?

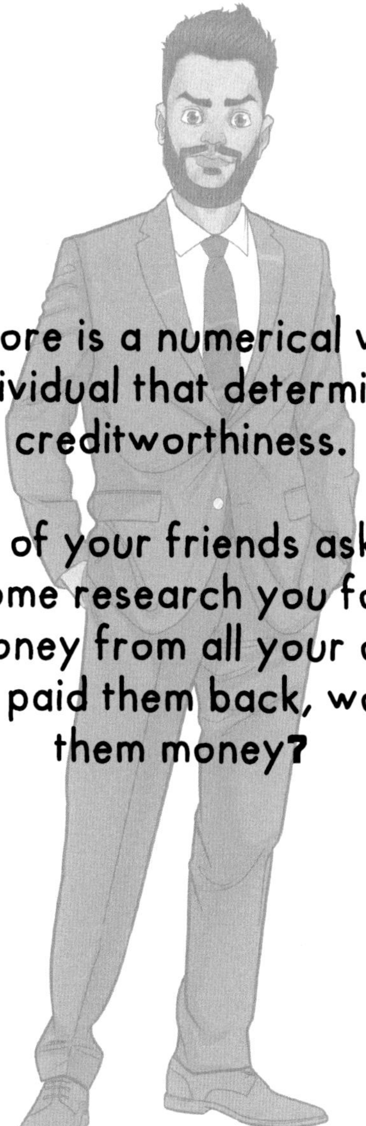

Your credit score is a numerical value assigned to an individual that determines your creditworthiness.

Let's say one of your friends asked you for a loan. After some research you found out they borrowed money from all your other friends and have not paid them back, would you lend them money?

WHAT IS INTEREST?

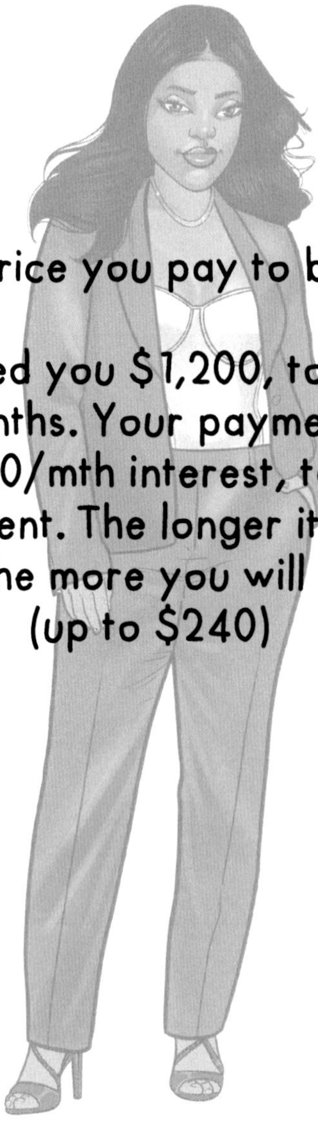

Interest is the price you pay to borrow money.

Let's say I loaned you $1,200, to be paid in full within 12 months. Your payment would be $100/mth + $20/mth interest, totaling a $120 monthly payment. The longer it takes to pay back the loan, the more you will pay in interest.
(up to $240)

WHY SHOULD I PAY MY BALANCE IN FULL & ON-TIME?

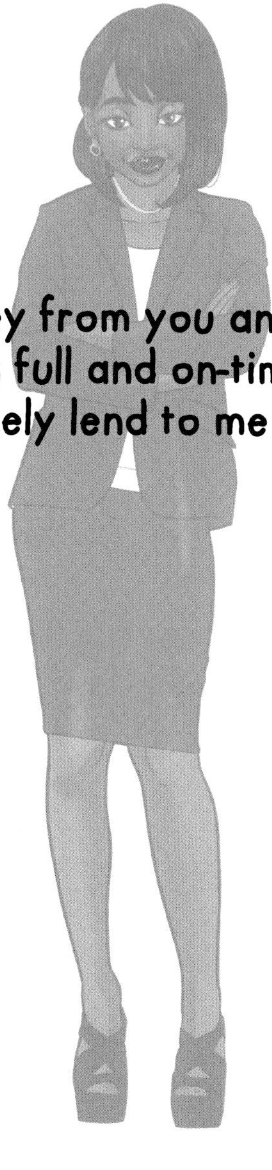

If I borrow money from you and pay you back with interest, in full and on-time...you would most likely lend to me again.

Made in the USA
Middletown, DE
26 September 2023